# Amazing Mandalas

## Adult Colouring for Relaxation

by J. Benson

# Amazing Mandalas

Mandalas are patterns with therapeutic value, used for centuries by Buddhists and other groups for meditation and to help reach a state of relaxation.

Amazing Mandalas contains twenty such Mandalas, designed specifically to help achieve a state of relaxation. Colour them in with a pen or pencil to help find your own state of inner peace and tranquility.

Accompanying each Mandala is a thought provoking message. These are optional, but provide something to ponder upon whilst colouring if desired.

Footsteps of success
are trailed by fading footprints
of failures past...

Amazing Mandalas
Adult Colouring for Relaxation
by J. Benson

We are successful
the moment we start towards
a meaningful goal.

Amazing Mandalas
Adult Colouring for Relaxation
by J. Benson

Anyone can talk,
but to listen is a gift
we should all exchange.

Amazing Mandalas
Adult Colouring for Relaxation
by J. Benson

People cannot fail,
they can only stop trying:
Continue, achieve.

Amazing Mandalas
Adult Colouring for Relaxation
by J. Benson

Absence of problems
does not lead to happiness.
Dealing with them does.

Amazing Mandalas
Adult Colouring for Relaxation
by J. Benson

The things we best teach
are the things we most needed
some point in our lives.

Amazing Mandalas
Adult Colouring for Relaxation
by J. Benson

We wear many things,
but that with greatest import
is our expression.

Amazing Mandalas
Adult Colouring for Relaxation
by J. Benson

Some believe they can,
some believe that they cannot.
Both are clearly right.

Amazing Mandalas
Adult Colouring for Relaxation
by J. Benson

Life without challenge
is life denied any chance
for one to achieve.

Amazing Mandalas
Adult Colouring for Relaxation
by J. Benson

Plan for the future,
learn from past experience,
live in the present.

Amazing Mandalas
Adult Colouring for Relaxation
by J. Benson

Stretched by an idea,
we can aspire to new heights,
new ways of thinking.

Amazing Mandalas
Adult Colouring for Relaxation
by J. Benson

A living is made
by what we get, but a life,
by what we each give.

**Amazing Mandalas**
Adult Colouring for Relaxation
by J. Benson

# Interlude

Amazing Mandalas
Adult Colouring for Relaxation
by J. Benson

# You have a voice

Are you enjoying your experience? The world wants to hear your voice! Whether you love or loath this book, your feedback can make all the difference when someone is deciding whether it's right for them! When you have the opportunity, please visit Amazon or your favourite social network and share your thoughts by leaving a review or rating of this book.

Thank you,


Jack

Only reflection
allows us to see ourselves
and fix our mistakes.

Amazing Mandalas
Adult Colouring for Relaxation
by J. Benson

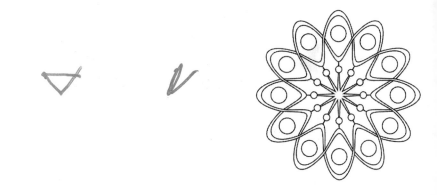

Strive to leave your mark.
Forge your own intricate path,
rather than follow.

**Amazing Mandalas**
Adult Colouring for Relaxation
by J. Benson

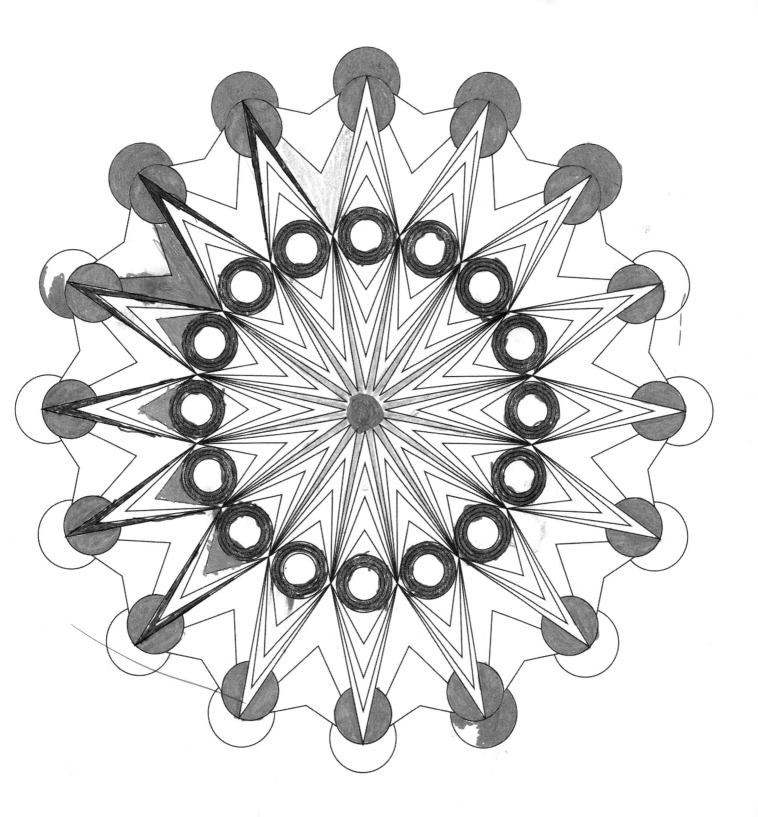

Things turn out the best
for people who make the best
of how things turn out.

Amazing Mandalas
Adult Colouring for Relaxation
by J. Benson

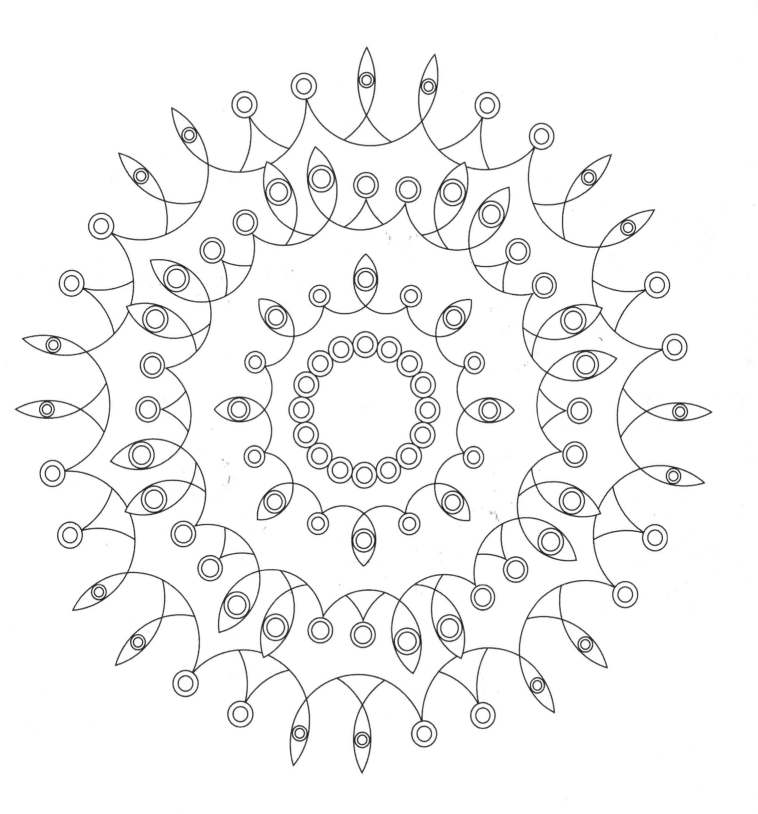

It's not what we have,
but how much we enjoy it
that forms happiness.

Amazing Mandalas
Adult Colouring for Relaxation
by J. Benson

Failure to plan,
living our lives recklessly,
is a plan to fail.

Amazing Mandalas
Adult Colouring for Relaxation
by J. Benson

Every minute
we spend in anger costs a
debt of happiness.

Amazing Mandalas
Adult Colouring for Relaxation
by J. Benson

What's ahead of us
is impossible to see
only looking back.

Amazing Mandalas
Adult Colouring for Relaxation
by J. Benson

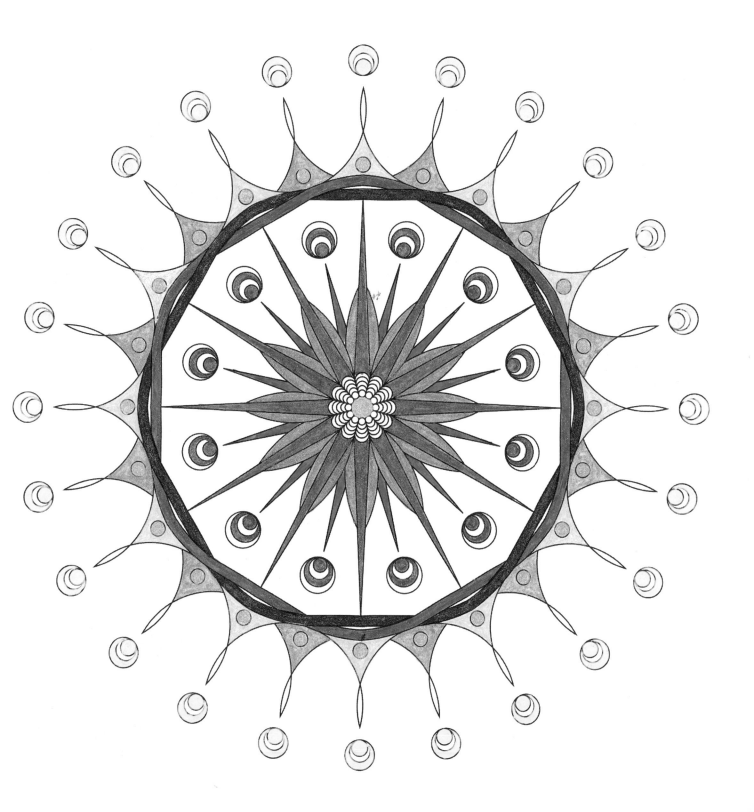

Sharing oft leaves less.
But with love, the more we share
the fuller our hearts.

Amazing Mandalas
Adult Colouring for Relaxation
by J. Benson

Now that you've completed this book, why not cut out your favourite patterns and share them with the people you care about...

Amazing Mandalas
Adult Colouring for Relaxation
by J. Benson

Printed in Great Britain
by Amazon.co.uk, Ltd.,
Marston Gate.